A
Conspiracy
of
Ravens

A Compendium of
Collective Nouns for Birds

Compiled by
Samuel Fanous

With illustrations by
Thomas Bewick

Bodleian Library
UNIVERSITY OF OXFORD

First published in 2014 by the Bodleian Library
Broad Street
Oxford OX1 3BG

www.bodleianshop.co.uk

5th impression 2020
Reprinted 2014, 2015, 2017

ISBN: 978 1 85124 409 6

Images originally published in Thomas Bewick's *History of British Birds*
(1797–1804).

Designed by Dot Little at the Bodleian Library
Typeset in IM Fell French Canon by Illuminati, Grosmont
Printed and bound in China by C&C Offset Printing Co. Ltd. on 120gsm
Chinese FSC® Baijin pure paper

British Library Catalogue in Publishing Data
A CIP record of this publication is available from the British Library

Foreword

I HAVE always enjoyed exploring the origins of birds' names. Some of them are helpfully descriptive. For example, little owl, long-tailed tit and pied flycatcher all do 'what it says on the tin'. Quite a few are onomatopoeic. Most of the crow family's names imitate their calls. Raven from *rraffen*, rook from *roork*, jay from *chay*, jackdaw from *chack daw*. They are more obvious if you say them with a Nordic accent! These are the names in common use by birdwatchers, but most birds also have 'folk names', handed down from generation to generation, or exclusive to a particular region. A few of them are still in use. Most species in Shetland go by their local name. *Bonxie* – great skua; *tystie* – black guillemot; *tirrick* – Arctic tern. I have also heard country folk call the green woodpecker a yaffle, and in Norfolk grey herons are often called cranes, which is very confusing since there are now a few pairs of common cranes in the county. But it is the really quirky and fanciful 'folk names' that you will find listed in books not unlike this one. Names like solan goose, old squaw, goatsucker and Mother Cary's chicken. In case you are wondering, that's gannet, long-tailed duck, nightjar and storm petrel.

However, the truth is I haven't heard anybody refer to these species by any of those names 'in the field'. Could they have been dreamed up on a boozy evening at the pub, or on those long winter nights, long before radio or television, when folk had to make their own entertainment, which perhaps included the popular family game of 'Name the Bird'? The single rule was that names must reflect some physical or behavioural feature of the species, and most of them did.

This is something that can't always be said about the collective nouns you are about to encounter, though it makes them no less entertaining. It is a documented fact that back in the Late Middle Ages there began among the hunting fraternity a game of inventing animal group names that became a fad; it became a challenge that continued for a couple of centuries or more. This was a chance to display wit and ingenuity; many were collected in *The Book of Saint Albans* (1486), a handbook on hunting, hawking and heraldry, which became very popular in the sixteenth century. Many were rather fanciful, and it is doubtful whether they were actually in common use at the time. But they were then reproduced in print and embellished by subsequent writers, so that now there are in existence many variations on collective nouns for animals, and a large number of them are for birds.

Just a few are still in common usage, albeit more by writers than naturalists. A *whisp of snipe*, a *charm of goldfinches*, an *exultation of skylarks* and a *murmuration of starlings* are all going strong. Some imply genuine ornithological observation – a *dance of cranes* – while I suspect a birder came up with an *invisibleness of ptarmigan* after a frustrating day tramping through snow in the Cairngorms. Perhaps the same baffled birder came up with a *confusion of warblers*. Others range from literal observation – a *crowd of redwings* – to frivolous wordplay – a *grain of sanderlings*. It is clear that this is a game that could run and run. In fact, why not a panel game on television?

The text of this book will amuse and bemuse, but the illustrations will delight. The first British 'field guide' didn't appear until the mid-1950s and yet Thomas Bewick essentially gave birth to the genre back in 1800. His wood engravings depict his subjects so exquisitely and so accurately that – even without colour – they are still peerless, both as an aid to identification and as art.

How about a *treasure house of Bewicks*?

Bill Oddie

A *Raft* of Auks

An *Orchestra* of Avocets

A *Colony* of Bee-eaters

A *Sedge* of
Bitterns

A
Merl
of
Blackbirds

A *Bellowing* of Bullfinches

A
Mural
of
Buntings

A *Flock* of Bustards

A *Wake* of Buzzards

A *Tok*
of
Capercaillies

A
Run
of
Chickens

A
Confusion
of
Chiffchaffs

A
Chattering
of
Choughs

A
Commotion
of
Coots

A
Swim
of
Cormorants

A *Leash* of Coursers

A *Box* of Crakes

A
Dance
of
Cranes

A
Spiral
of
Creepers

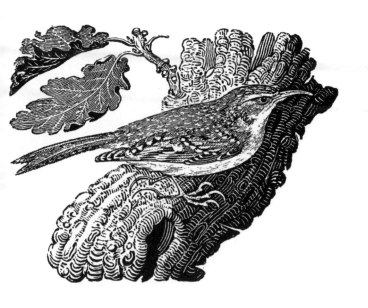

A
Crookedness
of
Crossbills

A
Murder
of
Crows

An
Asylum
of
Cuckoos

A
Curfew
of
Curlews

A *Trip* of Dotterels

A
Dole
of
Doves

A
Paddling
of
Ducks

A *Fling* of
of
Dunlins

An *Aerie* of Eagles

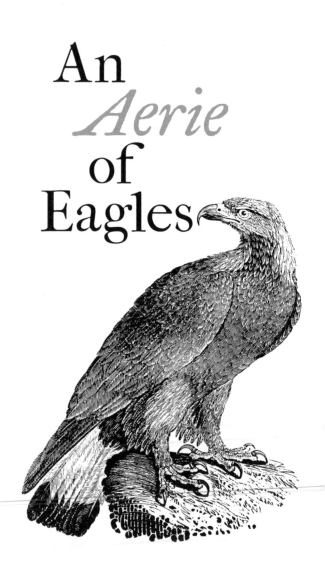

A
Quilt
of
Eiders

A *Heronry*
of
Egrets

A *Tower* of Falcons

A
Trembling
of
Finches

A
Swatting
of
Flycatchers

A *Gannetry* of
of
Gannets

A *Gaggle* of Geese

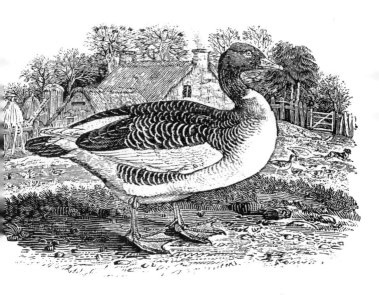

A
Prayer
of
Godwits

A
Charm
of
Goldfinches

A *Dopping* of
Goosanders

A
Glare
of
Goshawks

A
Water dance
of
Grebes

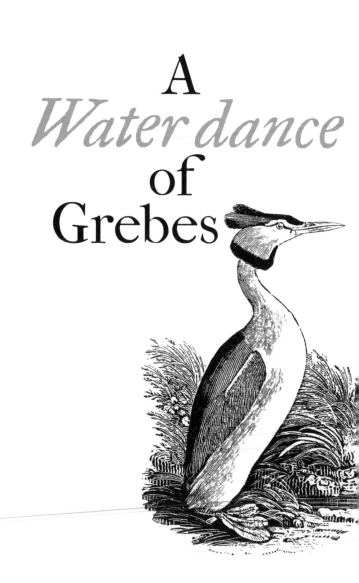

A
Drumming
of
Grouse

A
Bazaar
of
Guillemots

A
Confusion
of
Guinea fowl

A
Screech
of
Gulls

A
Harassment
of
Harriers

A
Posse
of
Herons

A *Nest*
of
Hobbies

A *Cry* of Hoopoes

A *Colony* of Ibis

A *Train* of Jackdaws

A *Scold* of Jays

A
Hover
of
Kestrels

A
Crown
of
Kingfishers

A *Soar* of Kites

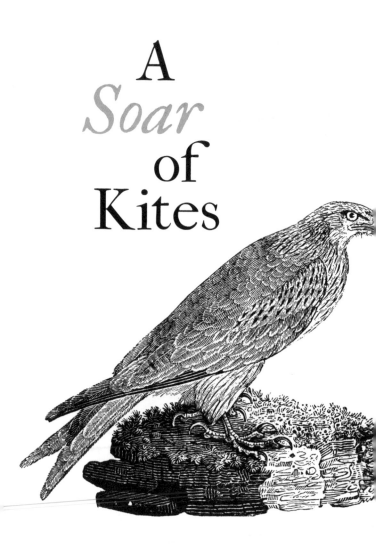

A *Flock*
of
Kittiwakes

A
Tangle
of
Knots

A *Deceit* of Lapwings

An
Ascension
of
Larks

A
Parcel
of
Linnets

An *Asylum* of Loons

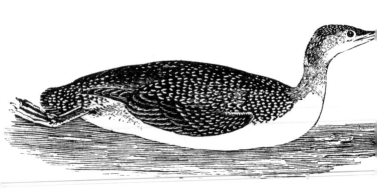

A
Mischief
of
Magpies

A *Sord* of Mallards

A
Circlage
of
Martins

A
Cast
of
Merlins

A *Plump*
of
Moorhens

A
Kettle
of
Nighthawks

A *Watch* of Nightingales

A
Suite
of
Nutcrackers

A *Booby*
of
Nuthatches

A
Pitch
of
Orioles

A
Duet
of
Ospreys

A
Wisdom
of
Owls

A
Parcel
of
Oystercatchers

A
Chatter
of
Parakeets

A
Covey
of
Partridges

An *Ostentation* of Peacocks

A
Rookery
of
Penguins

A
Cadge
of
Peregrines

A
Pantry
of
Petrels

A
Swirl
of
Phalarope

A *Nye*
of
Pheasants

A
Dropping
of
Pigeons

A *Knob* of Pintails

A *Wing* of
of
Plovers

An
Invisibleness
of
Ptarmigans

A *Circus*
of
Puffins

A
Rout
of
Quail

A *Conspiracy* of Ravens

A *Strop*
of
Razorbills

A
Gallup
of
Redpolls

A *Crowd* of
of
Redwings

A *Worm* of
of
Robins

A *Flight* of Rollers

A
Parliament
of
Rooks

A
Grain
of
Sanderlings

A *Colony* of
Sand martins

A *Fling*
of
Sandpipers

A
Squabble
of
Seagulls

An
Improbability
of
Shearwaters

A *Dopping* of
Sheldrakes

A *Watch* of Shrikes

An
Exultation
of
Skylarks

A *Whisp* of Snipe

A
Quarrel
of
Sparrows

An
Academy
of
Sparrowhawks

A
Runcible
of
Spoonbills

A
Murmuration
of
Starlings

A *Spell* of Stints

A *Muster* of Storks

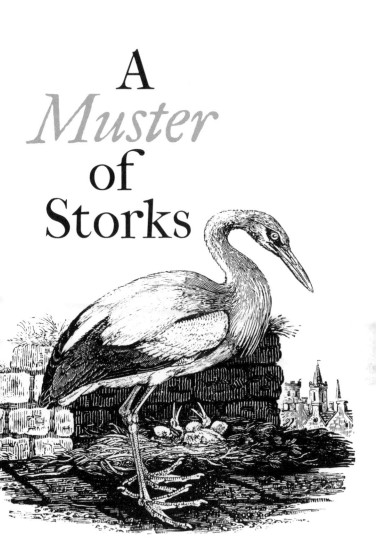

A
Kettle
of
Swallows

A
Lamentation
of
Swans

A
Flock
of
Swifts

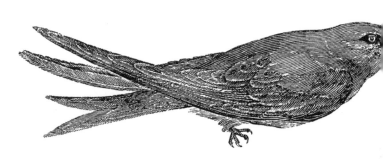

A *Spring* of of Teal

A
Committee
of
Terns

A
Hermitage
of
Thrushes

A
Banditry
of
Titmice

A *Raffle* of Turkeys

A *Pitying* of Turtledoves

A *Vortex*
of
Vultures

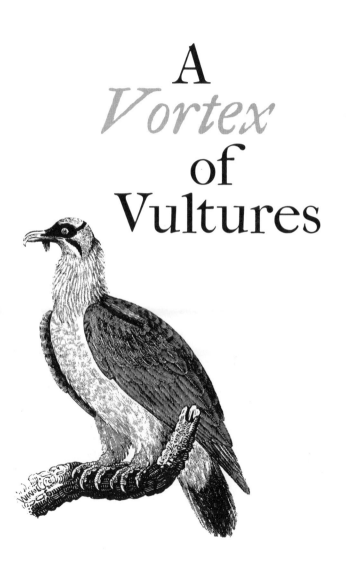

A *Volery* of
of
Wagtails

A
Confusion
of
Warblers

A *Sharning*
of
Water rails

A
Museum
of
Waxwings

A
Shaft
of
Wheatears

A *Fling* of Whimbrels

A *Fall* of
of
Woodcocks

A *Descent*
of
Woodpeckers

A
Chime
of
Wrens